Grandpa's Memories

of Main Street

Grandpa's Memories of Main Street

J. William Zoldak

STONEHEDGES

Grandpa's Memories of Main Street

J. William Zoldak

F I R S T   E D I T I O N

Softcover ISBN: 978-1- 954332-11-9
Hardcover ISBN: 978-1- 954332-17-1

Published by Stonehedges
OXFORD, MASSACHUSETTS

Dedication

In memory of my grandmother Aurelia Burger Zoldak and her ever present network of spies that enabled me to explore Main Street.

Dear Grandchildren,

I wrote this story about Main Street in my home town of Cornwall, NY, to give you and other readers an understanding of the vital role Main Streets played across America for past generations. I have included a map so that you can follow the location of each of the establishments as I talk about them. I also included old photographs of the buildings and other locations as they existed then.

Introduction

As the grandchild of a merchant on Main Street during the 1940's and 1950's, I was able to experience Main Street from a unique perspective. I spent many days, particularly in my early years, at my grandparents' tailor shop during the day while my father was working. My parents were divorced, and I lived with my father and grandparents. Later when I was about seven years old and my father had remarried, we moved to Clinton Street near the Episcopal church. From these vantage points, I experienced Main Street in a very special way.

The merchants were almost like one big family, supporting each other and sometimes competitive, but always dependent upon one another. Some were very close, meeting socially after business hours. Others were connected only loosely. Each not only recommended the others to their patrons but used them themselves for purchases of goods and services. In most cases, the family name was reflected in the business name on the door, and often the family resided in the same building.

There were no malls, big box stores, or supermarkets in small towns at that time. There were mail order companies, such as Sears and Roebucks and Montgomery Ward's available and some chain stores like JC Penny, Woolworths, and the Five and Ten Cent store in the cities, but most people shopped locally in the towns. Main Street was a busy place in those days. The following is an account of my thoughts, experiences and memories of those bygone days.

Main Street Locations

The Circle

- A. Park
- B. Brook
- C. New Cornwall National Bank
- D. Town Barn
- E. Chadeayne's Barn

Main Street Locations

1. Swenson's Insurance Office
2. Highland Fling (Goldsmiths House)
3. Stone's Agency
4. Zoldak's Tailor Shop
5. Bernicker's Barber Shop
6. Knapp's Feed Store
7. Cerasoli's Appliance Store
8. Hazard's Drug Store (Holloran's)
9. Canterbury Inn
10. . Johnson's Garage
11. Len Lewis's Garage
12. Telephone Company
13. Gus Newstrom's Delicatessen
14. US Post Office
15. Hey's Appliance Store
16. Birdsall's Grocery Store
17. Merritt's Florist
18. Cohen's Dry Good Store
19. Ushman's Hardware Store
20. The Fire Station
21. Cornwall National Bank
22. Clark's Meat Market
23. Glube's (Miller's) Variety Store
24. Schofield's Delicatessen
25. Edgar's Clothing Store
26. Herb Odell's House
27. Schriever's Ice Cream Parlor
28. Masonic Building
29. Ecker's Barber Shop
30. B and H Bar and Grill
31. A and P Grocery Store
32. Bobby K House
33. Alfred Cox Roe School Building

34. Sun Tags
35. Cornwall Garage
36. Methodist Church
37. Soldiers Memorial Park
38. Ring's Pond
39. Old Homestead
40. Baptist Church
41. Dr. Troidle's Office
42. Stanton Preparatory School (Town Hall)

22a Liquor Store

26a. Joe's Shoe Repair

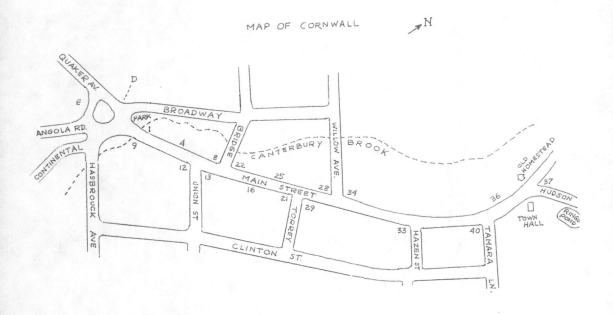

MAP OF CORNWALL   ↗N

⤳ *The Circle* ⤳

At the beginning of Main Street is a unique intersection where five roads merge on to Main Street. To make things even more difficult to explain to people unfamiliar with the area is the fact that the Canterbury Brook runs under this intersection as well. In the 1940's and early 50's there was no traffic circle or stop signs as there are today. Rather, there was a situation where cars and pedestrians entered and exited cautiously. There was, of course, far less traffic then, but it was still difficult to navigate.

AIR VIEW OF BUSINESS DISTRICT
CORNWALL, N.Y.

The areas adjacent to these entering roads had some features that are part of the Main Street story and worth mentioning. Between Main Street and Broadway was a tiny park with a foot path through it that could be used by pedestrians walking from one street to the other. Two things were important to me as a young boy about this little park. First, it allowed access to the brook that ran under Main Street. I spent many hours playing in that brook and getting soaking wet despite my best efforts. My grandmother would scold me

5

and forbid me from going back to the brook. That never worked. I was very young, perhaps, 3 or 4 years of age, when she would meet me at the entrance to the tailor shop saying, "you have been in the brook again haven't you". I would deny it even though I was visibly wet all over. Sometime afterwards I would ask her how she knew I had been in the brook and her response would be that a little birdie told her. I can't tell you how many hours I spent looking for that damn bird.

The second reason the park was important to me was that it contained a couple of very large Horse Chestnut trees. If you are not familiar with Horse Chestnut trees, they produce these wonderful nuts in the fall of the year. The outside of the nut is large and green with sharp spines all over it. As the nut ripens, the spiny covering falls off leaving an amazingly distinctive shiny red-dish-brown inner nut that is not edible but is wonderful in texture and conformation. These nuts are very collectible and almost jewel like in a child's imagination.

Between Broadway and Quaker Avenue was a dirt road that led to what was referred to as the Town Barn. This predated the Cornwall National Bank building erected in the 1950s. All of the operations of the town highway department were conducted from this site. The area was comprised of several sheds, a small office, and other rustic outbuildings. There were no fences or gates as you might expect in today's world, but rather just one large open, accessible area. I would often play in and around the sand piles, lumber, and discarded equipment. The men that worked there got used to me and seemed unbothered by my presence. Many years later, during my college years, I got a summer job working at the highway department (by then out on Route 32) and worked alongside some of the same men. It was a memorable job that I enjoyed very much.

Between the next two roads, Quaker Avenue and Angola Road, was a building that we referred to as Chadeayne's barn. I learned later that the building had been a prominent business (a general store) in its earlier days, but during my time, it was just an unused building. Behind the barn was a large, thickly covered brush field. This field later became the mall that stands there today, but it was quite wild when I was a boy. I'm pretty sure I remember hunting rabbits in this field.

After Angola Road came the Continental Road (same as today and important during the Revolutionary War) that followed the brook leading to Kenridge Farm, Route 9w, and the Black Rock Forest.

The last road on the circle was and still is Hasbrouck Avenue. This road has a bridge that crosses the brook and leads to the golf course.

Swenson's Insurance Office

This local business was owned and operated by Winnie Swenson. It was one of the most respected businesses in town. Everyone in my family, as well as the rest of the town, bought their home and auto insurance from Winnie. I also got my first auto policy there.

Winnie and my grandmother were good friends. She, along with other members of the business community, were part of my grandmother's spy network to keep track of me as I roamed the streets as a child.

Highland Fling (Goldsmiths house)

This old house was either owned or rented by the Goldsmith family. It was a dull yellow in color. I always thought that was fitting for a family named Goldsmith. I used to play with one of the Goldsmith boys until the house was sold, and they moved away. The new owner turned the house into a boutique type of shop called the Highland Fling. I remember this new shop caused quite a stir when it opened because it was the only one of its kind in town. It was quite popular although it didn't do much for me.

Stone's Agency

The Stone Agency was a real estate office, owned and operated by Elsie Melrose, (the daughter of W.H. Stone, the original owner) and her son Billy. There was never much activity in this building. I guess that was because most of their time was spent showing real estate out in the community. Alongside the building was a set of steps that led to the basement. I was fascinated with those steps. I would enjoy myself running up and down, using them as a prop in my imaginary adventures. They could, for example, be steps leading to the lower deck of a pirate ship or dungeon steps in a castle.

My grandparents and my father knew the Melroses very well. I think that my father may have grown up with Billy. I remember once years later when I was 15, my father arranged for Billy to teach me how to use the new spinning rod that I got for Christmas. He came to my house and showed me, in great detail, how it worked. I think spinning rods were a fairly new invention at that time. I still have that fishing rod some 60 years later.

Zoldaks' Tailor Shop

This establishment is one close to my heart because it was owned by my grandparents. As a boy, I would visit the tailor shop frequently and watch Old Jake (my grandfather) go about his daily routine. Every morning around 7 am and before the shop opened, several local men would arrive and socialize in the back room. I learned later that they were there, for among other things, to "bet the ponies" as they called it. The bets were made with a bookie, although I never knew the exact process. Around 9 am, Aurelia (my grandmother) would arrive, and the workday would begin. For her, this meant doing repairs and alterations for customers who left their clothing there for that purpose. Jake, on the other hand, measured customers and made customized trousers, coats and suits. Every phase of the tailoring business was handled in a professional manner at their shop.

The three rooms on the first floor of this brick building were set up to handle the tailoring business. The living quarters were upstairs. Behind the two large windows on either side of the front door, Jake and Aurelia sat behind their Singer sewing machines working all day long. Within the deep window bays, crowded in were plants such as Christmas cactuses and Jade plants as well as advertising posters. The words Mercantile Tailor were spelled out on the glass.

Behind Aurelia was a chest of drawers that contained every color and shade of thread imaginable. The spools of thread were all neatly placed in the drawers for easy access. Behind Jake was another chest of drawers with little wooden cubes containing buttons of every size, color and shape that you could imagine. Again, they were arranged for easy access. Near the back of the front room was a huge wooden table where the measuring and cutting operations were performed. In the middle room, accessible through a large open doorway from the front room, was a rolltop desk where most of the business transactions took place. Along the walls in this room were long rods where all the clothes were hung on wooden hangers. Some of the clothes were completed while others were in the process.

Through another doorway was the third room which was the most fascinating to me because it contained the steam press. Most of the time the steam press was quiet, but when Jake had enough orders to start the press, he would fire it up (literally) and press clothes until all the orders were filled. When Jake was pressing clothes, everyone in the neighborhood knew it. You could hear the sound of the steam being released several streets away, especially on the street behind the building. Along with the noise were great billows of steam that were amazing to watch. In the back of the building was a small yard surrounded by a low chain linked fence and behind the fence was a fast-moving brook. I mention the fence because it discouraged easy access to the hot steam as it left the building. The brook had another use. Because it was a natural trout stream, it provided more than one dinner for the family. Jake would simply use his fly rod to catch a couple of trout after work, and Aurelia would cook them up. All in all, the tailor shop was a fascinating place.

Bernicker's Barber Shop

Mr. and Mrs. Bernicker and their two children lived over the barber shop, and Mr. Bernicker worked downstairs performing the usual barbering services like haircuts and shaves. I'm sure that I got my first haircut there, but the one I remember most was the time my grandmother sent me for a regular haircut, and I requested a crew cut instead. I had long curly hair at the time, so I wanted to get rid of it. I was tired of being called "cute". After telling Mr. Bernicker what I wanted, he said that he needed to do something in the back room. I could hear him on the phone with my grandmother and when he returned, he sent me home. After a long discussion with my grandmother, I returned to the barber shop and got my crew cut. I think that was the only crew cut I ever got, but it did the trick, "no more curls".

One day as I was walking down the street, I saw a lot of commotion at the barber shop. When I checked it out, I discovered that the building was on fire. With smoke coming out of the windows, I saw young Billy Bernicker (a couple of years older than me) throwing clothes out the window to people below trying to keep them from being ruined by the smoke. That was the first time in my life that I ever experienced a house fire, and it left a lasting impression on me. I thought of Billy in a different way from then on.

Knapp's Feed Store

Knapp's Feed Store was an oldtime feed store where feed and other kinds of agricultural products could be purchased. There were two major sections. One was at the street level that was a rustic store front and open to the public. The other section was out back where the grain was stored and picked up or shipped. Old Mr. Knapp, the owner, always seemed to me to be a grumpy man. He seldom smiled and he answered questions with a one-word answer. Looks can be deceiving, however, and this story about him will tell you why I think so.

One day when I was perhaps 4 or 5 years old, I decided I wanted to buy a plant. I think I just needed a friend, and I thought a plant would fill that role. I didn't have much money at the time, only a dime and a nickel in my pocket. The only place that I knew plants were sold was at the feed store. I had seen a table set up with many different kinds of plants on display near the front of the store. So, I walked in to have a look. As I entered, old Mr. Knapp greeted me in his usual gruff voice. I told him I wanted to buy a plant, and he told me to go ahead and pick one out. I didn't know anything about the plants on display, and he didn't offer much advice. Thinking back, there were African violets, small Christmas cactuses, Jade plants and a few others that I can't remember. After long consideration, I decided to purchase one of the Jade plants. I picked it up and brought it to Mr. Knapp at the cash register. When I asked him the cost of the plant, he turned to me and said, "How much money do you have in your pocket?" When I showed him my dime and nickel, he immediately said in his usual gruff voice, "that will be fifteen cents". With that I thanked him and left the store with my new friend. Over time I realized, of course, what Mr. Knapp had done and thought of him in a much different way.

I kept that Jade plant for almost 50 years well into my adulthood. A friend named it George when my wife and I left it in Florida by mistake. After it was returned to us, we decided to keep the name. George unfortunately died a few years ago but I still remember him fondly. Jade plants only bloom with a tiny white flower about every 15 years and George bloomed at least twice.

Cerasoli's Appliance Store

This family owned business sold and repaired appliances. I remember walking by this store a lot but not much else. It was, however, quite popular, just not for me. My family generally bought their appliances from the other appliance store (Hey's) across the street.

Hazard's Drug Store (Holloran's)

Hazards was very old business that still exists today. In addition to pharmaceutical needs, Hazard's sold paper goods, newspapers, greeting cards and picnic supplies. In the front of the store was a striped awning that had to be rolled out every morning and returned at closing time. I remember old Bill, a local man who lived nearby, would do the job faithfully at both ends of the day using a crank that he brought out from the store.

Early in the morning, a newspaper truck would drop off a bundle of papers near the side door on Bridge Street. Several of the local patrons (mostly older men like my grandfather) would come by before the store opened and pull out a newspaper from the bundle and pay later in the day or by some arrangement. This was a well-accepted practice.

Inside near the front of the store was an old-time soda fountain where one could get any kind of soda and ice cream treat. My favorite was a root beer float (root beer and vanilla ice cream), but everything was available up to a large banana split. My friend Arnold and I would occasionally wait outside the store until his uncle would arrive to buy a newspaper. After checking the horse racing section his uncle would be in either a good mood or a bad mood, depending upon what he saw. When he was in a good mood, we would step forward, and he would often buy us a root beer float to celebrate his good fortune. When he was in a bad mood, we got out of there in a hurry.

Canterbury Inn

The Inn was located on the bank of the Canterbury Brook, thus its name. It was a tavern in those days, patronized by mostly local men. I'm not sure if any food was served there, but if it was, it was a very limited menu. My grandfather often purchased his beer there, and when I was old enough, I did as well. The Lowenbrau beer they had on tap was quite memorable.

The brook, after crossing under Main Street at this point, ran through the town parallel with Main Street and behind the stores.

Johnson's Garage and Len Lewis's Gas station

These businesses pumped gas and repaired cars. Lewis's Sunoco station was the older of the two. Len's grandfather once operated a blacksmith's shop on these premises but, as times changed, it became an auto repair shop. My family patronized this station for gas and all auto repair needs. I later worked with Jackie Lewis (Len's son) at the highway department. Jackie was a good friend and, at times, a mentor during my teenage years.

The other station was owned by Fred Johnson and serviced cars and pumped gas as well. As time passed it became a Dodge dealership and was purchased by Billy Bernicker, the son of the barber across the street.

Fred Johnson's daughter, Nancy and I were in the same youth group at the Methodist Church. She and her best friend Karen, stabled their horses at Pop Cowton's Stable on the outskirts of town. I also frequented that stable during my teenage years. We were all good friends.

Telephone Company

The telephone company building always seemed out of place to me because it was just a concrete building with no character. I guess important things took place there like switchboard operations, but I mostly ignored it, as did most people, I think.

Gus Newstrom's Delicatessen

Gus and his family ran this as a very successful business. I don't remember much about this deli other than the overwhelming impression of cleanliness.

US Post Office

The post office was a relatively new brick building where one of my class-mate's (Irene) mother worked. I remember going through the wastepaper baskets there looking for unusual stamps during my stamp collecting stage. I found mostly 3 cent stamps which was the cost of postage then, but occasionally I found what I thought of as a gem. Irene lived on one of the side streets not far from the post office, and I remember that she owned a big black dog (Blacky) who often slept in the middle of the road in front of her house. When a car would come down the street, it would simply drive around him. There were no leash laws in those days.

Hey's Appliance Store

Hey's Appliance store was in a building that had been the Grand Hotel in an earlier era. There were a couple different owners of this business over my years, but I remember Hey's particularly. My family bought all their appliances there, like stoves, refrigerators, radios, and, later, after they became available, television sets. It always struck me as interesting that our small town could support two appliance stores across the street from one another.

Birdsall's Grocery Store

This was a very small store by today's standards, but it had almost everything a family needed in the way of groceries. It prided itself on customer service. We shopped there as well as at the A and P Store further down the street.

Merritt's Florist

Merritt's Florist is now a very old business, but I remember when it first started. It actually started further up Main Street near my grandfather's tailor shop. My uncle Harry, who always enjoyed flowers, worked with the Merritts in the beginning. In a relatively short time, this shop became very popular. After a year or two, Mr. and Mrs. Merritt purchased the brick building where it is now located. I remember on one occasion I was asked to deliver an arrangement to a family on Clinton Street. The person answering the door gave me a generous tip for my efforts which I thought was great. That was my first and only delivery job.

Cohen's Dry Goods Shop

This shop always seemed crowded to me with all kinds of everyday articles in a very small space. My grandmother would often send me there to pick up something. I'm pretty sure that Mrs. Cohen was part of my grandmother's network that kept track of me as I roamed around the town.

Ushman's Hardware Store

Every town in the 1940's and 50's had a hardware store. There was no Home Depot or Lowes in those days. Mr. Ushman owned and operated this store which often seemed disorganized, but he seemed to know where everything was in it. The store later included a small lumber business located behind the store with an entrance from the street behind (Clinton Street). I didn't know Mr. Ushman very well, but we did buy our hardware needs there, as did everyone else.

The Fire Station

We had a volunteer fire department that was well equipped. Many of the men in the community were volunteers including some from my family. A strong social organization was also associated with the fire department. To raise money each year, they had a three-day event called the Fireman's Fair.

At this annual summer event, the street in front of the fire station was closed in the evening to all traffic. Side streets were used to reroute the cars. The fair was an event that everyone looked forward to. It was kind of like a carnival, but with volunteers. I have many fond memories of those summer nights. As I got older, I helped Stanley and Pop Cowten with the pony rides. It was quite enjoyable lifting the little ones on to the horses and leading them down the side street and back. The cost, as I remember, was 25 cents.

As I got into my teenage years, I would bring a date to the fair. I remember on one occasion I tried to win a big teddy bear at one of the booths for my date. It didn't work out, so I went back later that night and bought it from the fireman that was running the booth. When I told him why I wanted it, he was glad to sell it to me at a very fair price.

Cornwall National Bank

This was an attractive brown brick building that looked like a bank. Everyone in town used this bank as it was the only one in the area. The usual banking activities took place there, like savings accounts, checking accounts and business accounts, as well as mortgages, etc. I think I probably opened my first account there. In those days, the bank was open from 9am to 3pm Monday through Friday. That was all. Hence the term "banker's hours".

Clark's Meat Market

This business was one of the oldest in town. At the time that I was a child, it was owned and operated by Everett Clark, but it had been in his family for generations. This was a real oldtime meat market with sawdust on the floors to soak up the blood and a big old scale to weigh the meat. As you stood at the counter waiting for your order, you could look into the back room and watch the butchers cut the meat from these large carcasses that hung on hooks from the ceiling. The store was always cold to keep the meat fresh. My grandparents often sent me there to pick up an order, which I enjoyed thoroughly. On one occasion I was told to pick up a ham bone so that my grandmother could make pea soup. I was quite surprised to find that the bone was free of charge. The soup was great.

Liquor Store

The liquor store was very popular among the adults in town but I had very little interest in it. I'm sure some of my family members shopped there from time to time.

Glube's (Miller's) Variety Store

This store was first owned by the Miller family as a confectionary store and later by Mr. Glube as a variety store. The Millers had a grandson who was my age that I used to play with from time to time. When Mr. Glube bought the store, he enlarged it to the point that he carried every product imaginable. His motto was "if we don' have it, we will get it". A patron could buy anything, from a package of gum, to clothing, to small appliances or a jackknife. I bought my first shotgun in this store and the ammunition that went with it. Mr. Glube would often barter on price if that was needed to close a transaction. It was a unique store indeed.

In the 1920's, this building was the original location of my grandfather's tailor shop when he first opened his business. He later sold the building to Mr. and Mrs. Miller and moved to the brick building further up Main Street.

Schofields's Delicatessen

Schofield's Meat Market and Deli as the name implies sold meat and deli products. I remember the long glass counter that the Schofields stood behind as they took orders. Mrs. Schofield ran the business alone after her husband passed away. She and my grandmother were good friends, as I remember. I think she was also part of the network that kept track of me.

Edgar's Clothing Store

Edgar's, was a small clothing store that carried mostly women's apparel. The front windows were always filled with upscale fashionable clothing. While the ladies of town shopped there, it didn't have much appeal to me. In my early years, I remember this building being the local post office before the new post office building was built further up Main Street.

Herb Odell's House (police)

Herb Odell was the only police officer in town. All crime in our community was handled by Mr. Odell, who had a unique way of handing out justice. For example, if a mischievous young boy were to steal flowers from someone's garden or perhaps damage the property of one of the businesses in town, he might capture the culprit and hand him over to the grandparents. This kind of justice was far worse than going to jail, I can assure you, or at least that's what I've heard. Mrs. Odell and my grandmother were good friends. They even played Bingo together every week. She was another of my grandmother's spies.

Joe's Shoe Repair

This little shoe repair shop was run by Joe Mastrota a long-time resident in the town. I had very little contact with the shop, probably because I grew out of my shoes long before they needed repair. It was a fascinating little shop though because you could look through the big windows in the front and watch Joe in his leather apron working on the shoes. Joe was a fisherman so sometimes he would hang a sign on the front door that read "Closed Gone Fishing". Being a fisherman myself that sentiment always appealed to me.

Schriever's Ice Cream Parlor

This was a carryover store from a bygone era when confectionary stores were popular. I barely remember it but do remember that the ice cream was outstanding. My grandmother, on occasion, would give me some money to get a treat from this wonderful old shop.

Masonic Building

The Masonic Building was a fairly large one-story building that never seemed to have any activity around it. I guess it was used for meetings at night when I was not around. My uncle was a mason so he probably went to meetings there. It always seemed to me that this building had a peculiar shape with a skirt around it from the main part of the building to the sidewalk. I think I used to walk on that skirt.

Ecker's Barber Shop

This barber shop was patronized by many of the men in town, but I went to a different barber, so I don't have any memories of this shop. I do remember standing in front of it one evening and witnessing a drunk driver crashing into a parked car as he tried to turn onto Torrey Lane. Herb Odell showed up and took care of things. No one was injured.

B and H Bar and Grill

This local establishment served patrons alcoholic beverages every evening. It was also the home of one of the town's most important civic organizations. The Chicken Thieves Detecting Society (the name is another story) met there to plan their annual events all year long. Two of the events they sponsored, and that I participated in as a child, were the annual town wide

Easter Egg Hunt and the Fishing Contest. These were strictly for children and totally free. These men may have had their vices, but they were certainly generous with their time and resources. I don't think I am the only person who remembers these events. I was at the very first Fishing Contest held at Rings Pond and received a prize for catching the largest cat fish. I had less success at the Easter Egg Hunt, only occasionally finding an egg.

A and P Grocery Store

This chain grocery store was very popular during the 40's, 50's and beyond. The one in our town was very small and located in an old building that had been converted to house the store. There were two long aisles where all the groceries were shelved. The floors were made of wood and they rolled up and down as many floors do in old buildings. One of my friends (Bobby) lived in the house next door. His yard was adjacent to the A and P, so I was able get a good view of the back of the grocery store. I remember taking and eating the fruit that was no longer fresh enough to be sold. Mr. Van Leuven, whose daughter Roberta was one of my classmates, managed the store. He knew we took the fruit but never said anything. The over ripe bananas were particularly good.

I can also remember with great enthusiasm taking some of the large cardboard boxes that were discarded from the store and building wonderful forts behind the store. We would play for hours in these boxes, sometimes in the rain.

Alfred Cox Roe School Building

This old wooden framed building once housed a school, but when I was a child, it was a residence located on the corner of Main Street and Hazen Street. In the winter, as children, we would sled down Hazen, stopping just before entering Main Street. If that sounds dangerous, that's because it was. At the time, an elderly lady living in the house would open the window and scold us when we got too close. I never knew her name, but she knew ours (Jeff, Mike, Bobby, Gary, and me). I was living on Clinton Street near the Episcopal Church at that time.

I learned to ride a bicycle while living in this area using the bike of my friend. The following Christmas I got a brand-new bicycle of my own and in the spring while riding down Hazen Street onto Main Street crashed it into an oncoming car. The person driving the car turned out to be a Doctor on his way home from the hospital. He treated me on the scene for cuts and bruises and then insisted that I go to the hospital. My grandmother arrived at the hospital about the same time I did. The spy network at work again, but this time I was thankful because I was a little scared.

Sun Tags

Sun Tags was a small variety store with a soda fountain or lunch counter attached. This store never seemed very busy. That made me wonder how it stayed in business. I think the people who lived in that section of town must have patronized it enough to keep it alive.

Cornwall Garage

This building housed the local bus company. The buses that transported the public to nearby communities as well as the school buses that took the local students to school were all housed and serviced in this building. The business was owned and operated by Harry Keevil. There was also a tiny coffee-shop like establishment attached. When I got older, I would sometimes stop in for a sandwich and a cup of coffee at this little shop. I think it was there mostly to give the bus drivers a place to relax between routes but it was also open to the public. I liked listening to the old guys, especially old Ernie (Marvin), reminisce about their trips to Newburgh.

Methodist Church

Although I attended Saint John's Episcopal Church on Sundays, I also had a close connection to the Methodist Church. My grandmother didn't know this at the time, or she probably would not have approved. My first encounter at the church was in the summertime when I was playing along the brook (same brook that ran through town) behind the church building. I was with a friend, and we noticed activity in the hall attached to the church. As we moved closer to look, the side door suddenly opened, and women appeared asking us what we were doing. Figuring that we were caught and in trouble, we simply said that we were curious about what was going on. To our surprise, she invited us in, gave us a snack and asked if we wanted to participate in the Bible School that they were conducting. We said yes and spent the rest of the morning along with the other children (some of whom I knew from school) doing fun activities. I came back each day for the rest of the week until the program was over. My grandmother never knew.

When I was older, I joined the youth fellowship there, mainly because I was invited by some young ladies who were involved in the program. Over those years, I enjoyed many wonderful activities at this church. As it turned out, several years later, I became a Methodist when I married the minister's daughter. That was 55 years ago.

Soldiers Memorial Park and the Old Homestead

. I always memorialized these two sites in my mind because of their historical nature. I would occasionally visit them and always think of their significance. As a child, I loved to see the old cannons but never understood why they were there until I got older. The importance of the Old Homestead came to me earlier, probably because I was told that George Washington slept there. I mean who wouldn't be impressed with that. The people from the historical society have told me since that he never did, but I didn't know that back then. As far as I was concerned, this was the museum part of town and sacred in nature.

Baptist Church

The Baptist Church was a relatively new building that was set back from Main Street. Next door was the parsonage where Reverend Houser and his family lived. His youngest son (Gary) and I were good friends.

Dr. Troidle's Office

Dr. Troidle. was our family doctor. He was a general practitioner who had office hours in a section of his house. His wife, who was a piano teacher, also gave lessons at their home. It was a very interesting arrangement whereby they shared the same waiting room. If you were waiting to see the doctor, you might be sitting next to someone waiting for a lesson, and you would probably hear piano music in the background. Village doctors in those days also made house calls, but routine health issues were generally handled during these office hours. I didn't take music lessons, but Mrs. Troidle did know me by name. Perhaps another of my grandmother's spies.

Stanton Preparatory Academy (Town Hall)

This brick building was set back from Main Street and housed the Stanton Preparatory Academy. The Academy was a preparatory school for the U.S. Military Academy at West Point. The building and the property around it later became the Town Hall and the town park. I remember once when I was, perhaps, seven years old (1950) helping a man collect bricks from a demolished building that had been located between the present Town Hall and Ring's Pond. He was going to use the bricks at his home. I'm not sure what he was going to use them for, but I do remember that he made several trips with his car. I think that was my first paid job. I got $1 for my efforts.

Over the years I spent many hours on this property as a Boy Scout in an adjacent building, playing tennis on the courts nearby, and just running up and down the hill behind the Town Hall. Although the swimming pool was constructed during my years, I never swam there. By then I lived outside of town and swam in an old swimming hole instead.

Ring's Pond

Ring's Pond is not officially on Main Street (Hudson Street), but it's worth mentioning because of its importance to the town. My earliest memory of Ring's Pond was before the town owned it. From the street, it was almost hidden from sight because it was surrounded by high grass and brush. I once, when I was very young, made my way through the tall grass to the edge of the pond and saw two very large yellow perch (at least a foot long) swimming in the shallow water. Later, of course, I remember fishing there each spring and summer, and the wonderful times ice skating on the pond with friends in the winter.

The 4th of July Parade

While this annual event had no connection with any particular building, it was important to the history of Main Street. I can remember as a small child standing in front of the tailor shop watching the 4th of July parade pass by. It seemed like it took forever for it to come into sight and then when it was over, I remember thinking that it wasn't long enough. As I got older, I, too, participated in it.

Every year a theme was selected, and all of the organizations in town got involved by sponsoring a float. The floats were decorated with great care and pulled or driven down the street on the day of the event. For example, our Boy Scout Troop 20 was involved several years. I also had the exciting privilege of riding horses in the parade. One year I remember riding as a cowboy using one of the horses from Pop Cowton's Stable and borrowing a real cowboy shirt from a family friend because I didn't own one. Another time I was dressed as a Patriot during the American Revolution. This time was particularly memorable because I had an important role during the pageant. The pageant in those days took place after the parade at Donahue's farm in the lower village (Cornwall on the Hudson). Every year a reenactment of the Battle of Fort Montgomery was performed as part of the program. My part was to gallop into the encampment with news that the British were advancing. I took this as an important role. Besides, I got to gallop my horse up the hill in front of a large audience. Historically, of course, the Americans lost this battle so it always seemed strange to me to celebrate a failed effort. As I got older the importance of the battle made more sense. The Patriots lost, but the British were stopped from advancing up the Hudson River.

After the parade, the pageant, and the Battle of Fort Montgomery were over and darkness set in, the fireworks began. The fireworks on Donahue's farm were particularly impressive because they were set off at the base of Storm King Mountain causing amplified sounds and echoes off the mountain. No other fireworks display in my life time has ever measured up to those at Donahue's farm.

⟿ *Final Word* ⟿

I hope with this rather long description of Main Street and my interaction with it, that you, the reader, and especially my grandchildren. can understand the uniqueness it offered. Main Streets still exist in small towns across this country, but not in the same way. I'm sorry to say that those days are gone forever. Perhaps my sharing these experiences can give some understanding of how special those times were.

Love as always,
Grandpa

CONTRIBUTORS

Walter Earl
   Photos on pages 6, 8, 13, 16, 18 top, 20 top, 20 bottom, 21 bottom, 24, 25, 26 bottom, 28, 32, 36 bottom.
Cornwall Historical Society
   Photos on pages 7, 10 top, 14, 15, 17 bottom, 18 bottom, 19, 21 top, 23, 26 top, 27, 29, 30, 31.
Zoldak Family
   Photos on pages 5, 9, 10 bottom, 11 top, 11 bottom, 17 top, 22, 33, 34, 36 top.
Nancy Loux
   Map of Cornwall
Lorrie Kulhavy
   Photo editing

ACKNOWLEDGEMENTS

Nancy Loux for her sketch (map) of Main Street, Cornwall, New York.
Lorrie Kulhavy for editing the old photographs.
Jonathan Young for his technical support.
Walter Earl for the use of his family photo collection.
The Cornwall Historical Society for the use of their photo collection.
The Zoldak family for the use of their family photos.

Printed in the USA
CPSIA information can be obtained
at www.ICGtesting.com
LVHW082345281023
762327LV00005B/160